Clouds

A collection of Wandering Thoughts

Shagun Kandpal

India | USA | UK

Made with ❤ on the BookLeaf Publishing Platform
www.bookleafpub.in
www.bookleafpub.com

Dedication

I want to dedicate this book to my mom and her unceasing faith in my abilities.

Preface

I am a person who always thinks, and thoughts rush into my mind regardless of my will. Sometimes, it troubles me relentlessly. I needed an outlet to calm myself and to channel my thoughts productively. I used to write a diary entry, but it was not always feasible to take my diary around. On the same note, one day, I was conversing with my younger sibling, Ishita, on a random topic I do not remember. And I concluded that I should start writing poems to channel my thoughts. I just need my phone to sum up my emotions. This idea is working wonders for me. I am calmer and productive than ever before.

I have named my first book *'Clouds: A Collection of Wandering Thoughts'* because this book was born from my wandering and aimless thoughts, just are the clouds in the sky. Clouds flutter aimlessly in the sky. It felt like the most appropriate name for my book.
Certain trains of thought are responsible for all my poems, but you, readers, are free to interpret the poems according to your issues that you are most reminiscent of in the moment.

I hope this book provides you with a wonderful reading experience.

Acknowledgements

Showing Gratitude is never enough for me. It reminds me of the countless blessings I am showered with every day.

First and foremost, I show my gratitude to my god who has been sailing my ship for eternity. I can never thank my mother, *Abha*, enough for the love and care she has showered me with. She has protected me with every ounce of her being. I sincerely show my appreciation to my siblings, *Vaishali* and *Ishita*, who are always present to trouble and support me through everything. A shoulder I can always lean on, I found my second mother in my aunt, *Ronika*. The four pillars of my life, *Payal*, *Samriddhi*, *Anmol*, and *Nandani*, would have been non-existent without you guys. A big thanks to my grandparents for the sarcasm they instilled in me. I thank all of my dear friends and well-wishers for supporting me through my hardships. I am deeply grateful for the support of my loved ones. At the end of thanking my dear ones, a big pawstruck thanks to my cat, *Piku*, is a must on the list, although he is unbothered as always.

I sincerely acknowledge *BookLeaf Publishing* for the

platform and the tremendous opportunity I have been provided with to present my ideas to everyone. Your team's support and expertise have been invaluable.

1. My Mother

I don't know what I did,
To get a mother like you.

Is it a blessing that God showered on me?
Or god himself came into existence?

I don't know how do you have every answer to my
troubles.
I don't know how you can understand the depth of both
my happiness and sadness.
I don't know how you have the ability to become me in
moments of my intense emotions.
I don't know how you can forgive everything I ever did
to hurt you
And still show up for me stronger than ever.

I don't know how you have faith in me and my potential
more than I ever had in myself.
I don't know how when something good happens to me,
I am happy
And you are happier.

I don't know how when something bad happens to me,
I am cracked

And you are broken.

I don't know how when we both suffer together,
You are able to gather that scattered strength to support
us both.

I don't know how you are able to show up as an angel
whenever I need you.

It is said that whoever you meet in this lifetime are not
new souls.
You always knew them.
Mom,
Maybe I saved you multiple times in your past life?
In our past life,
Maybe you were my mother and I was your daughter?
Maybe I was your mother and you was my daughter?
Maybe we were sisters?
Or maybe you were always the one who has been saving
me since eternity?

I don't know how we are able to meet each other so
deeply in every life,
Even after our body crashes and ends in the soil.
And we have no identity and our memory vanishes
How do our souls still recognize each other in every life?

Is it because some souls are meant to travel together?
No matter how many births they take,
They stay intertwined with each other
They travel together
Till their journey ends into higher realms of frequencies
Or till the souls journey to meet and converge with the
creator?

I don't know if this is all true,
But if it is,
I wish to pass my every birth alongside you my savior.

2. Divergent

Calling out my wild side that was once existing,
Lost it in the worldly struggles I was facing
Many of the nightmares I see are not mine to own
But has to be seen since I decided to walk on the path
alone.

A feeling hits me every now and then, I can't relate to it
But it is mine, I know, as it never left me since the day it
arrived.
I don't know if it is my friend or foe, but it is loyal.
It never goes.

I am forever conflicted about the two paths that I foresee,
One takes me to a materialistic getaway,
While the other makes me float in the spiritual realm.
I want to get rid of the dilemma of it.
But this dilemma is so close to me that I can't find myself
existing without it.

Maybe this was the bittersweet truth that I had to face
To get together with my lost wild side that once was
existing.
Lost it in the worldly struggles I was facing.

3. Law Of Forgiveness

A weird word came into existence
Forgive,
Is it for others or for myself?
Is it meant to calm others or myself?
Is it meant to heal others or myself?
Is it meant to save others or myself?
Is it meant to deepen bonds with others or myself?
Questions keep prevailing endlessly in a loop,
Everything shoots arrow at the explanation that all of
forgiveness is for me.
Maybe it does, maybe it does not
The arrow of forgiveness only deepens the wound,
scrapping the scab again and again
Until you are kindred with the pain, it hurts.
I don't know how a word that is meant to cure only
hurts,
Is it teaching to endure the pain or let it all go?
But how either way is kind to me?
But I still do or atleast try.
A path I don't want to travel ever
But every path of mine ends in forgiveness,
Whether I want to or not.

4. Feline

Always adored felines,
Domestic or stray
A creature bound to its ways and unbothered by the hate
it faces.
No lies, deception, or a mask on its face
So real that it sometimes seems fake.
It builds a deep desire in me
To be as carefree as they seem
Never under any pressure to please others
Is solitary in function but out of desire, no fears
unleashed.
Just me and me
Maybe this is why I adore felines
And sometimes abhor me
Perhaps I am as polar as they seem,
and unpolar equally.

5. Mourning Mirror

Waking, turning, crying in the middle of the night,
Woke up from a dream troubling me.
As soon as I left the realm of turmoil, a thought hit me
Was it a nightmare or sadness building inside me?
Instantly, Sadness looked me in the eyes tearfully,
Was it that much of pain it was suffering from?
I tried to console it unsuccessfully for a long time.
I realized that sadness had a face like me
I stared for a long time and saw only me in her.
Unacknowledged, underrepresented, and misinterpreted
as always
But why a lot of Un- and mis- for myself
Who was it that made me feel this way?
Or it has always been me, assaulting me, for the
unanswered questions life threw at me
In the life's struggle, I made a foe out of a friend, and I
finally saw her now
Staring at her eye to eye now
It was always me looking at me as a stranger.

6. Seat

Looking for a seat somewhere,
That is saved just for me.

No struggle to fight for it,
No struggle to retain it,
No struggle to claim it,
No struggle to define it,
Just mine to belong,
With my name engraved.

Although reaching to the chair
Is the heftiest and the most painful experience.
Like walking on a floor on bare feet,
With shattered glass scattered.
But a will, a wish, a hope stays
That somewhere this painful walk ends.

Haven't reached the chair but
Gradually psyche flips
Hope is turning into belief,
Wishing is peaceful.
And pain is not so painful.
I know I am close by
To my chair,

To my seat,
To my space.

Any direction I travel,
As far as I go,
Beyond the concept of space and time,
That space is there
That comfort is there.
That peace is there.

That seat is out there,
Waiting for me to find it.

7. To The Ones I Love

A prayer from the deepest of my existence:

" I will never wish that you don't have troubles,
Or you don't have struggles,
 Or you don't have phases of sadness.

But I will always wish that these things bring out
responses that make you the person you are meant to be.
I hope you never stay the same.
I hope you meet yourself first before anyone.
I hope you are never deaf to reasons, blind to magic, or
mute to exist.
I hope the one you know the most, understands the
most,
Feels the most,
is always you.

I hope all your felt and unfelt Purposes come to life
naturally,
Like breathing, it fills you with hope to move on,
Like food, it gives you the strength to kill the monsters
under your bed,
More importantly, heal the issues that haunt your soul,
I know it will hurt in the process, but I wish you keep

walking,

It will all be worth it at the end of human reasoning,

Trust that voice from the innermost pit of your consciousness.

It knows.

It always knows. "

8. Painful Memories

If you were given the choice to forget every painful
memory that exists right this moment,
Will you do it?

An instant response of yes might appear brought upon
by to human mind of ours,
But as you ponder on the question, an urge of denial
rushes upward.
A reason emerged?
Breathe that reason...
It tells you a lot about you.

9. Web Of Heart

A weird web spun in expectations and hope,
Trapping lies, deception, and greed every now and then,
A mechanism born to filter out odds and grays and
destroy them
Has, with time, turned into a doorway.
That allows everything and everyone to pass by into the
deepest core.
Catching every small prey in the web and letting the
most dangerous ones into the deepest core.
Odds turn malignant and a catastrophe in the deepest
core
With no cure, no healing, no filter,
One day, the weight of unwanted prey on the web
overwhelms, and the web breaks.
The mechanism snapped and cracked
A door borne out of fear formed at the entrance
Trapping the odds forever.

Soon the life dies, leaves dry, hope dies, and birds fall
No life left in the uncared-for mansion.
Abandoned with a curse and a cure, still trapped in the
broken web, sticking to its walls.

10. Healing

Healing is not something we chase,
It is a hidden realm inside us.
It needs a mantra to open the door,
And unleash the magic.

It is ours and known,
Still, we need to explore and find it.
As it is a mirage,
Hidden within a mirage in a desert.
It is easy and simple to find,
And it is the difficulty it possesses.
Cause we are blinded by fears and disbelieves,
Growing exponentially through generations of existence.
Only one solution stays.

Sit with yourself alone to find it,
Sit with your grief to find it,
Sit with your anxiety to find it,
Sit with your anger to find it,
Sit with whatever that troubles your soul to find it.

That is when the mirage vanishes.
That is when the magic wand swirls
That is when the hidden realm elevates,

From the depths of our souls,
To evaporate everything blinding us.

11. Complete Puzzle

Thousands of alternate versions of events exist,
With thousands of consequences that stem from them,
Probability of favorable outcome falls in the ditch
Then how does our wish come into being?
How does our labor earn the fruits to savor?

Somewhere, someplace, someone exists...
That turns the impossible probability of an outcome into
reality...
Just faith and grace that everything turns out even is
needed.
Although not every wish comes true,
Not every push bore fruit.

But slowly and gradually, every piece of the puzzle falls
into the right place,
Broken pieces eventually form a picture.
That is how universe makes wishes come true.
For every being that is breathing.

***Note: The inspiration for this poem came from the belief
in the divine powers of the universe.***

12. Timeliness Of Love

What makes you stay longer than destined?
Is it love for the person, or that innate desire that
something magical will happen and turn that nightmare
into a fairytale?

How do you decide that the dreaminess has hit the road
And now it is time to honor the deadline?
Maybe you have fallen in love with the potential
And is blind to the reality that befalls upon you.

It is hard to respect the deadline,
But honor the sweet memories that helped you in the
beginning.
Don't wait for the sweetness to turn sour.

I hope both the ends realize that it is time to mend things
before everything shatters.

But if it doesn't happen....
I hope both the ends are left with the capacity to heal.

On the latter end of hope,
Maybe it was a wrecked ship on the shore from the
beginning,

But you denied to remove your rose-tinted glasses and
continued to watch it as a 5-star cruise on a voyage.

Let that Titanic sink,
Not because the love was lacking,
It happened as the other aspects became more than the
love ever was.
Not because the ship was a great piece of architecture
and had a low probability of sinking.
It happened because of the belief that the ship could
never sink.
Because that gut feeling knows from the start that a few
lifeboats can't save everything.

It sank deep into the ocean.
But it was always meant to sail.
It was always meant to flourish.

13. Salmon

Letting go,
Turn into a salmon on a quest.
A quest to turn every wound into a scar,
As now it all feels like a salmon swimming against the
flow of a river.
Drained, wrecked, swimming to its death.
The time has run out,
So we have to let it all go.
Again, swimming in the river that gave you birth.

You have to swim,
Even if you were once seemingly thriving in the faraway
ocean,
Let it stay as a place away from home.
Even if it once had the potential to turn into a beautiful
song,
Let it stay as noise.
Even if it was once a beautiful script to be reckoned,
Let it stay as a play that never materialized.
Even if it was once your favorite pair of earrings,
Let that one lost piece be lost somewhere.
Even if it was once synchronicity of events for you,
Let it all stay in entropy now.
Even if it was once a beautiful piece of art,

Let it stay as a broken vase in the corner of your store
room.
Even if it was once your go-to favorite movie, you could
have watched again a thousand times,
Let it stay that heartbreaking movie tape that never left
its case again.

Cause the prelude makes you see salmon swimming to
their death,
And the end makes you see it swimming to rejuvenate
the life cycle.
So, you have to turn into a salmon on a quest,
Again, swimming in the river that gave you birth.

*Note: The inspiration of this poem has come from the life
cycle of a Pacific Salmon and the author's beliefs. In
short, all Pacific salmon starts their lifecycle in
freshwater like streams and rivers, migrate back to the
ocean, then return back to their birthplace in freshwater
to lay eggs and die soon after.*

14. Empath

Correspondence with empathy is a nightmare,
Sometimes you feel the weight of the issue
Sometimes you add extra weight to a feather-light issue
Sometimes you feel the intensity of others' emotions,
The intensity that is unknown to even the one
experiencing it.
Sometimes you can feel the guilt of others for hurting
you,
Sometimes it makes you take away the pain of all others,
even at the cost of your peace.
Sometimes you are understanding of the ones who
stabbed you,
Empathy makes you a forever forgiver,
Unable to hold grudges for the ones that break you.
Is it a superpower or a masked curse?
Does it help you understand more, or it make you
unrealistic?
Does the Earth realm work this way, or the realm that
exists beyond our understanding?
I guess we'll never know,
And it is better this way.

15. Trauma And Love

The easiest thing a person can ever do is giving and receiving love.
But with passing time and stacks of trauma,
The most difficult thing a person can ever do is loving someone.

The weight of trauma is so overwhelming that it scares the kid inside a person.
A kid who only wants love is deprived of it all,
Because their adult exterior is scared of vulnerability.
The capability of trauma always attacks the capacity to love.

A person can move mountains in anger, but can't push the idea of being scared of love.
Denying love is the greatest deception to our souls.
The complexity of trauma is winning over the simplicity of love.
It is heart-wrenching, but a bitter truth no one is willing to face.

Since when has rolling a boulder off the mountain top become difficult?
Since when has pushing a boulder to the peak become

easier?

I guess breaking hearts is easier than mending them.
It is.
It always has.
It is easier to hide behind a rock than fighting your
demons.

16. Patience

Everything takes its time to happen,
It won't happen early,
It won't happen late
It won't happen even if you are desperate
It won't happen even if you are on top of your scale of readiness.

It crochets at an appropriate pace.
A pace not set to suit your mind,
A pace set to honor the route you take.
It troubles you endlessly,
Not because you need it immensely,
It only troubles you,
Because the unpredictability of events scares you.

Your neediness of the conclusion,
doesn't skip the route it has to take.
The emotions are to be felt,
The troubles are to be felt,
The instability is to be felt,
The pain has to be felt,
Every undesired push is to be felt,
Before you are handed over the peace.

Before you are handed over the vision of the bigger picture.

17. Ocean

Like an immense ocean,
You are existing in 3-dimensions,
With an equally calming and scary surface,
Ending in the uncharted depths, impossible to
completely fathom.

The blues, the dark, the cold taps as the depth increases,
The monsters lurking in the dark are haunting every
section.
The mega scale of existence turns the harmless creature
in the dark,
Into the evil monster with razor teeth, finding its
helpless victim.

The waves in the ocean,
Reminds of the rampancy at the bottom fighting to reach
the surface.
Scared of the vastness,
We live ashore on the sunny beaches,
Away from all the dangers and the opportunities that the
ocean depth offers.

The monsters are still living,
They are still thriving,

Away from the visible range of beaches.
Maybe the darkness of the ocean needs to be addressed,
As happily as you address the sunny beaches.

Maybe the monsters in the sea are not as scary as they
seem.
Maybe the darkness is not as overwhelming as it seems.
Maybe it is all that dark side of the moon that we have
never seen.
But it is still the part of the moon that lights up the night
sky.

18. Limitless

How can I limit myself when I am eternally limitless?
I don't want to be in a small color palette when I can
dance among the multitude of colors.
Somewhere inside me, two voices echo,
One obsessed with my growth,
The other one always frightened that something bad
might happen.

The two voices fight endlessly to secure a win,
Every fight ends in a draw,
I secretly bet on the voice that wants my growth.
It never wins,
It never loses, too.

I have faith that my voice that wants the best out of me
wins,
I suppose it is winning,
As I am smothered with a newfound hope.
Everything is falling in the right places.

How can I limit myself when I am eternally limitless?
I suppose I don't need to ponder on this question
anymore.

I suppose there is nothing I need to be scared of
anymore.

19. Tones of Black

What do you do when you fall into the deepest, darkest water with no light around?
You sink deeper and deeper,
You can't differentiate the phase of darkness as all tones of black are the same.
But when you sink deeper and deeper,
All tones of black are visible,
All tones of black are felt,
All tones of black turn to void without knowing.

Soon, you realize you are not in the ocean.
You are in the deepest pit of your mind.
You are admiring the darkness that prevails.
But what happens when you don't have the will to swim upward anymore?
Should you try swimming or stay where you are?

20. I Accompany Me

I enjoy my company more than any other being in existence.

I sit with myself talking about every topic I can,
I am open to hearing my thoughts as often as I want to.
There is no such thing as experiences differ from person
to person with me.

The me in me knows every happy moment and tragedy
that life threw at me.
The me in me has experienced every life moment in the
pool of emotions with me.
The me in me has faced every dilemma and has come to
a solid path with me.
The me in me has witnessed my every battle with the
demons.
The me in me has fought every battle with the demons
alongside me.

The me in me has the same battle scars I got while
fighting the demons I faced.
The me in me is the person who is always there to lend
me an ear when no one is around me.

I was never alone with me.
I am never alone with me.

21. Cherishing The Present Stage

Currently in a headspace where I don't want to fall for the maybes.
Currently in a headspace where I don't want to hurt myself anymore.
Currently in a headspace where I don't want to revisit the past that broke me.

Cause I want to respect my emotions more than anything.
Cause it doesn't hurt when I am looking at the sunset and not at my shadow falling behind.
Cause you can't trip and fall from a rock that is behind you.
You only trip and fall from a rock that is behind you when you turn around and walk through that path again.

Cause looking at a glass half-full with water was always better than seeing it half empty.

9 789370 924215